K.S. in Lakeland

MICHAEL HOFMANN

K.S. in Lakeland

New and Selected Poems

THE ECCO PRESS

New York

The Ecco Press
26 West 17th Street
New York, NY 10011
Published simultaneously in Canada by
Penguin Books Canada Ltd., Ontario
Printed in the United States of America
FIRST EDITION

The author wishes to acknowledge the editors of the
following publications, in which some of these poems,
previously uncollected in book form, have appeared:
*The Agni Review, The American Scholar, Antæus, Boston Review,
Honest Ulsterman, London Review of Books, Mother and Child, New Poetry II
(Quartet), New Statesman and Society, The New Yorker, The Paris Review,
Partisan Review, Poetry, Poetry Ireland Review, Soho Square (Bloomsbury),*
and *Times Literary Supplement.*

Library of Congress Cataloging-in-Publication Data

Hofmann, Michael.
K.S. in Lakeland : new and selected poems / Michael Hofmann. —
1st ed.
p. cm. — (Modern European poetry series)
I. Title.   II. Series.
PR6058.0345K17   1990   89-39902 CIP
821'.914 — dc20

ISBN 0-88001-197-1

Contents

III

IV   (ENDZEIT)

Part I

Looking at You   (Caroline)

Having your photograph on my bedside table
is like having a propeller there . . . My friend
did his project on the Gallipoli Offensive—
with a proud Appendix of family heirlooms:
irrelevant fragments of German aircraft.
I covered the Russian Revolution (the only
lasting consequence of the Great War,
I argued) but with nothing more tactile
than a picture section—central feeding
in tsarist times: cabbage soup and black bread,
the Eisenstein-faced peasants with red pupils . . .
I take your unnaturally serious expression
and coax it into a smile or a glum look—
dotted lines pencilled in for velocity—but
you still won't budge. Then I imagine your
stasis as whir, movement in perfect phase,
just before it starts walking backwards . . .
All the walks here lead into the autobahn:
they are dual carriageways for pedestrians,
with wire bridges over traffic unusually
quiet in the snow. A blue signpost marks
the distances: Nürnberg 100; Wolfsburg
(home of the Volkswagen) 200; Berlin 500 . . .

The pioneers of aviation were never alone—
they named their machines after their loved ones.

Up in the Air

The sky was breaking, and I felt little less numb
than the alcoholic devotedly spooning
pâté from a tub; than the divorcée's station wagon
with its dog-haired sheepskin dogseat;
or the birds barking in the trees to greet the day . . .

There was a grey heron standing on a green bank.
'Soul survivors' spilled out of the *Titanic*
in their once-fluorescent sailing whites.
You only live once. The record sang 'My Girl,'
but that was a lie. She only shucked my cigarette packet,

as she danced before my eyes like the alphabet,
mostly like the letter A . . . I was Ajax,
I had stolen another man's captive, slaughtered sheep
like a maniac, counted my friends till
I fell asleep, now I would have to swim for it

in the greasy, yellow, woolen waves . . .
The bass drum went like a heart, there was a pillow
curled in the bottom of it for anchorage.
Our finger-joints shook in the free air,
sheep's knucklebones dicing for the seamless garment.

Three hours flat out on the hotel candlewick,
blunting my creases, then off to the airport
with its complement of tiny, specialized, ministering
vehicles. I sat over the wing, riveted, wary,
remembering ring fingers and flying kites.

A Floating City

'Un seul être vous manque, et tout est dépeuplé'
—Lamartine

After the card-players, the cuba libre drinkers
and the readers of two-day-old newspapers,
there are the night strollers, pastel shades down the
                                                    bobble-lit
Atlantic esplanade, by the small roar of the waves.

We saw the passenger liner put in for the afternoon,
then put out again: a floating city, heading South,
then pulling a slow turn, end on to the shore,
and backing North-West for the Azores or the
                                              shipping-lanes –

a wide and wasteful curve, elegiac and deceptive,
like that of your plane (and its decoy), that I followed
standing in the jetstream as they lifted away,
penny-pinching Britannias on their chartered tails . . .

The place was demolished in an earthquake and rebuilt
on a new site: built down, having learned its lesson,
wide and flat, built for cars. – With you gone out of it,
it seems destroyed again, and rebuilt to less purpose.

I stand on Avenue Mohammed V like a crowd hoping for a
                                                    motorcade.
When the King comes to stay, he's like an earthquake,
living with the one thing his paranoia can live with,
the migrant population he calls an entourage.

Day in the Netherlands

Commuting tourists, we retire
from the city in the evening
to a house in the floral suburbs,
Linnaeuslaan, the street sign giving
the dates of the great botanist . . .

From the fibreglass perfection
of a fly-boat, we saw Amsterdam's
thinnest house; prison-cells built into
the supports of a bridge, their
window-bars called Swedish curtains

on the German commentary tape;
the station constructed on thousands
of wooden piles. The Shell building—
that funny look in its windows
comes from the gold dust in them . . .

We are so overfed that if we
had supper as well, we could
only quarrel afterwards. So we
skip it and sit by the canal
in the last warmth of the year.

For the first time, we dare to talk
about our past, contiguity that
preceded love, and kept it
at bay . . . My room opened off yours,
it could have been a cupboard.

Touring Company

In your cavalier fashion, you leave your
small change on my floor. You keep pots of it
at home.—It feels sick to be alone again.
Like a charlady I shake my head at the dust,
and scrape it into pieces of knitting
with my fingers.—On the *Nautilus* there was
apparently never any dust, as all their air
came out of cylinders. But then Strindberg
or Hamsun, or another of those northern mis-
anthropes, writes that dust consists almost
entirely of dead human skin . . . Captain
Nemo's men can't have decomposed as we do.

Yesterday, you played five small male parts
in *Macbeth*: four cowards and a murdered child—
a friend drew a red line across your throat
with his dagger. I sat in the front row,
worrying about the psychological consequences
of being murdered every night for a month . . .
And the blood seeped into our private life;
that of the stars was washable, but yours was
permanent for economy. It pales on my sheets,
souvenir of your lovely blush . . . When you left,
you forgot your vanishing-cream—my biker,
spark-plugs mixing with tampons in your handbag!

Ancient Evenings

(for A.)

My friends hunted in packs, had themselves photographed
under hoardings that said 'Tender Vegetables'
or 'Big Chunks', but I had you – my Antonia!
Not for long, nor for a long time now . . .

Later, your jeans faded more completely,
and the hole in them wore to a furred square,
as it had to, but I remember my hands
skating over them, there where the cloth was thickest.

You were so quiet, it seemed like an invitation
to be disturbed, like Archimedes and the soldier,
like me, like the water displaced from my kettle
when I heated tins of viscous celery soup in it

until the glue dissolved and the labels crumbled
and the turbid, overheated water turned into more soup . . .
I was overheated, too. I could not trust my judgement.
The coffee I made in the dark was eight times too strong.

My humour was gravity, so I sat us both in an armchair
and toppled over backwards. I must have hoped
the experience of danger would cement our relationship.
Nothing was broken, and we made surprisingly little noise.

A Feminist Ballet

The colour in life is supplied by women . . .
She bought a pair of baggy workman's overalls,
cut them up, & dyed the pieces separately
in all the colours of the rainbow: Roy G. Biv.

Thomas Mann's Aschenbach, a stream of ashes,
longed for the arrival of his dinner-suit,
a uniform of moral & cultural stability,
the belief in an unimpeachable Absolute.

(When he started wearing younger clothes,
rouged his cheeks, & painted his lips like
sickly twin cherries, he was only making
things easier for the mortuary beautician.)

So it is with the captains of German industry;
an aerial photograph shows them in small groups,
one hand nursing a drink, the other in a roomy
trouser-pocket. Over their hearts, they wear

handkerchiefs impeccable as their credentials.
Like anarchists, they see things in black & red.
—A society closed to women, they stand on
the solid ground of a brightly submissive carpet.

Pavement Artistes

after E. L. Kirchner

His women are birds of paradise, cocottes:
stiletto-heeled, smoking, dressed to kill.
They wear veils to cage the savagery

of their features. Like the motherly pelican,
they are plucked bare—except their hats,
which are feathered and tipped like arrows.

They live together on a green traffic island.
Berlin Zoologischer Garten—*tristes tropiques*!
The station clock measures their allurements.

Their control of outlying stairways and arches
is ensured by their human architecture.
The gothic swoop of shoulder, waist and hip.

For men, they are something of a touchstone,
distinguishing them into the two categories
of policeman and clown . . . You can see both types

strolling down the boulevard, bowler-hatted
and terrified of shadows—sometimes testing
the street's temperature with a long foot.

Museum Piece

The room smells of semen. The leather curtain
that hangs in the doorway to keep the men
from the boys is now flapping like a ventilator . . .
People crowd in to see the erotic drawings.
Yonis in close-up like a row of fingerprints.
—Hokusai's hairfine precipice technique
applied to pubic hair. Fingers do the walking,
tiny feet wave in mid-air. His white ladies
groan under the weight of swollen members.
. . . The four estates of Japanese society—
fishermen, actors, courtesans and samurai—
mixing it. Following no useful calling,
anonymous in their nakedness, lovers clutch
each other. We might be watching ourselves,
dizzy men and women without designations . . .
We jostle in the dark for a better view.

Nights in the Iron Hotel

Our beds are at a hospital distance.
I push them together. Straw matting
on the walls produces a Palm Beach effect:

long drinks made with rum in tropical bars.
The position of mirror and wardrobe
recalls a room I once lived in happily.

Our feelings are shorter and faster now.
You confess a new infidelity. This time,
a trombone player. His tender mercies . . .

All night, we talk about separating.
The radio wakes us with its muzak.
In a sinister way, you call it lulling.

We are fascinated by our own anaesthesia,
our inability to function. Sex is a luxury,
an export of healthy physical economies.

The TV stays switched on all the time.
Dizzying socialist realism for the drunks.
A gymnast swings like a hooked fish.

Prague

Between Bed and Wastepaper Basket

There hasn't been much to cheer about in three years
in this boxroom shaped like a loaf of bread,
the flimsy partitions of the servants' quarters,
high up in the drafty cranium of the house.

All things tend towards the yellow of unlove,
the tawny, moulting carpet where I am commemorated
by tea- and coffee-stains, by the round holes of furniture –
too much of it, and too long in the same place.

Here, we have been prepared for whatever comes next.
The dishonest, middle-aged anorexic has been moved on.
The radio-buff is now responsible for contact
in the cardboard huts of the British Antarctic Survey.

(His great antenna was demolished here one stormy night.)
The tiny American professor is looking for tenure.
On occasional passionate weekends, the vinegary
smell of cruel spermicide carried all before it.

Familiarity breeds mostly the fear of its loss.
In winter, the ice-flowers on the inside of the window
and the singing of the loose tap; in summer,
the thunderflies that came in and died on my books

like bits of misplaced newsprint . . . I seize the day
when you visited me here – the child's world in person:
gold shoes, grass skirt, sky blouse and tinted, cirrus hair.
We went outside. Everything in the garden was rosy.

Prefabs ran down the back of the Applied Psychology Unit.
Pigeons dilated. The flies were drowsy from eating
the water-lilies on the pond. A snake had taken care of
the frogs. Fuchsias pointed their toes like ballerinas.

My hand tried to cup your breast. You were jail-bait,
proposing a miraculous career as county wife
and parole officer. We failed to betray
whatever trust was placed in us.

Tales from Chekhov

They are in a hotel in a foreign country
where the morals are different. It is their
first time away from home, and it is not
going well. He, as a leading industrialist,
has implosion on his mind: the destruction
of their vacuum by the external pressures
of this place—the laughter and fertility,
arrogant *machismo*, spicy cooking. He hopes
his British restraint will see him through . . .
But there are internal forces to contend with
as well. Their marriage has crept safely past
its "accursed seventh year"—without children.
. . . Husband and wife fall back on each other.
He obscurely feels and resents foreign blood
in her; it allows her to feel at home here,
in this ruined, pregnant city—and keeps her
from understanding him. He becomes cynical.
Other women he sees begin to look attractive . . .
but he gets nowhere. Meanwhile, she discovers
the extinct possibilities that every woman has
in her past—and mournfully explores them.

Their respective tourism exhausts them both.
He helps her downstairs with his knuckle cocked
against the small of her back like a trigger.
It is a last, sarcastic form of etiquette.
—Ironic kidnapper with nonchalant victim,
they go down to the bar together . . .

Monsters of the Deep

We could never understand how it worked:
their relationship was unfathomable.
We told each other Ovidian tales
of blackmail and sinister domination.
Our curiosity was a small boat,
which stopped at a plotted latitude
and dropped anchor, while we projected
ourselves over the side in dry-suits
and bathyspheres, with torches and harpoons,
leaden-footed frogmen of the imagination.

Epithalamion

'The old couple, owners of this crabby, marine hotel,
sit in their armchairs like Canute, talking of

nothing but the circling death of their Great Dane.
Out on the terrace, the proud, demented peacocks

crack their breakfast eggs on cement. Our honeymoon,
seedy and British. Character to proficiency –

no shy, intrusive maid, bringing us champagne . . .
In church, ladies' hats outnumbered our friends.

We were the minister's "young friends". He told us
about love and called us "Richard and Stephen".

Were we the Princes in the Tower? The whole edifice
rested on us, on her stiff dress and my tie-pin.

No one could help us. With his shock of white hair
and his mangy dog-collar, the minister arraigned us,

yelping against the flesh like a dog in the manger,
importuned, blundering, resentful, exploited.

He thought he was performing a rescue service –
a fireman at midnight, two cats up a tree in flames . . .'

De-militarized Zone

My cigarette glows, and your bones snap
in the dark. Not another torture scene . . .
Like the men in the trenches, I don't smoke,
I don't want to give myself away to the enemy.
—But the tobacco is mixed with saltpetre,
to keep it burning . . . I curse them quietly,
the nervous little cackles of flame in my lap.

It doesn't make sense. You know where I am—
on the chair, carefully holding an ashtray
in my other hand, and listening to you . . .
After our tired argument in your parked car,
we are relaxing from the ordeal of each other;
unwinding, in our different ways.—And you,
you're double-jointed and subject to backache.

I am familiar with your calisthenics,
and the order in which you perform them—
a series of stretches and Yoga positions.
I was told the fluid explodes in the cartilages
and turns to gas. Anyway, it restores you . . .
On good nights, I rub my hands together
and take away the static from your eyes.

Not tonight, of course . . . But even so,
I hear you undressing, in this small room
most of your things land on my feet, and you
get into bed. We weren't talking any more,
but then you ask me to come to bed as well,
and, thinking what a blessing it is to be allowed
to forget our differences like this, I comply.

On the Margins

Hospitality and unease, weekend guests
in this Chekhovian rectory painted a frivolous
blush pink. It is comfortable and fallen,
as though run by children, but with an adult's
guiding hand for basics, food, warmth, light . . .
At other times, what conversations, what demeanours!
I stare at myself in the grey, oxidized mirror
over the fireplace, godless, inept, countrified.
The distance disappears between rooms and voices.
Stuffy and centripetal, I tag after my hosts,
talking, offering 'help', sitting on tables
or leaning ungraciously in the doorway.

We drove twenty miles to buy roses, to a stately home
behind a moat and a pair of netted Alsatians.
The shaggy, youthful master of the house
was already on to his second family. His little boy
must have guessed. He had the exemplary energy
of the late child, working on his parents' stamina,
boisterous and surexcited, running to fetch us
prayer books, one at a time, they were so heavy.

Back here, I feel again spiritless, unhappy, the wrong age.
Not to be condescended to, still less fit for equality.
I quarrel with you over your word 'accomplished',
and then slink off upstairs to make it up . . .
We hear the hoarse, see-saw cries of the donkeys
grazing in the churchyard, mother and daughter,
and the first mosquitoes bouncing up and down,
practising their verticals like a video game. Next door,
his green clothes hung on pegs, Eric, the rustic burr,
is taking a bath, whistling and crooning happily
in his timeless, folkloric voice. I pat your nakedness.
In evil whispers, I manage to convince you.

Body Heat

This evening belongs to a warmer day—
separated clouds, birds, bits of green . . .
We wake late, naked, stuck to each other:
the greenhouse effect of windows and bedclothes.

Fifty years late, you finish *Love on the Dole*.
—Who knows, perhaps it can really be done?
The Boots hair setting-gel no longer works;
your pecker is down. The underdog's leather jacket

is here to stay, the stubborn lower lip
of the disconsolate punk . . . The poor hedgehogs,
they must help each other to pull off the leaves
that covered them while they were hibernating.

Changes

Birds singing in the rain, in the dawn chorus,
on power lines. Birds knocking on the lawn,
and poor mistaken worms answering them . . .

They take no thought for the morrow, not like you
in your new job. – It paid for my flowers, now
already stricken in years. The stiff cornflowers

bleach, their blue rinse grows out. The marigolds
develop a stoop and go bald, orange clowns,
straw polls, their petals coming out in fistfuls . . .

Hard to take you in your new professional pride –
a salary, place of work, colleagues, corporate spirit –
your new *femme d'affaires* haircut, hard as nails.

Say I must be repressive, afraid of castration,
loving the quest better than its fulfilment.
– What became of you, bright sparrow, featherhead?

Diablerie

Your ringed hands clutch your elbows. In your arms
is someone else's child, a black-eyed baby girl
dressed like His Satanic Majesty in a red romper suit:
a gleeful crustacean, executing pincer movements.

Aerial Perspective

Where the picturesque collides with the strategically
important, in some dog-eared, dog-rose corner
of Cornwall or Suffolk, there's a clutch of airbases,
and a weekend cottage called Boeing's Rest . . .

I can only hear the big AWACS aircraft
homing back in the fog across the North Sea –
tailplanes like leg-nutcrackers, and ridden by
their great, rotating, white-striped black toadstools –

but no doubt they can see us blips, as they can see
the blind gophers chewing up the putting-surface,
and the discarded copy of *Pull* or *Weapon* lying in a hole
in the road: men at work, a reassuring sight.

From A to B and back again

The Northern Line had come out into the open,
was leaving tracks like a curving cicatrice.
There was Barnet, my glottal stop, trying hard
to live up to its name, colloquial and harmless and trite.

The place was sunny and congested, brick and green trim,
it had the one-of-everything-and-two-butchers
of a provincial town. First, I dropped into
the maternity hospital by accident . . .

The porter was an analphabet, but together
we found your name, down among the Os,
and there you were, my brave love,
in a loose hospital gown that covered nothing;

pale; on an empty drip; and eager to show me
your scars, a couple of tidy crosses
like grappling hooks, one in the metropolis,
the other some distance away, in the unconcerned suburbs.

Part II

Going East

Anthracite and purges, the old upright carriages
of the *Deutsche Reichsbahn*, of old Imperial Germany . . .

Among the bird-cherries and ceramics factories
on both sides, the frontier is a moment of distinction.

The crossing-point is the good count Gutenfürst:
where Alsatians defend the Republic like Cerberus

protecting Hell, their leashes noosed to a wire –
vibrant, free-running, holding on like grim death.

Furth i. Wald

(for Jan and Anja T.)

There are seagulls inland, extensive flooding
and a grey sky. A tractor stalled in midfield
between two goals. Mammoth sawmills collecting trees
and pulping them for furniture and wallpaper . . .
These strips of towns, with their troubled histories,
they are lost in the woods like Hansel and Gretel.
Counters at peace conferences, they changed hands
so often, they became indistinguishable, worthless.
Polyglot and juggled like Belgium, each of them keeps
a spare name in the other language to fall back on.
Only their wanton, spawning frontier tells them apart,
an arrogant line of wire in an electric clearing.
(A modern derivative of the civic myth of Thebes:
the oxhide cut into ribbons by cunning estate agents,
and laid end to end; so many towns called Cuernavaca . . .)
—At other frontiers, it may be a long tunnel instead,
too long for you to hold your breath. At halfway,
the texture of the concrete changes, and the lights,
but you can't say where it is brighter or safer . . .
Nations are irregular parcels, tight with fear.
But their contents have settled during transport.
Grenzflucht. Perimeters that are now deserted and
timid, the dream-wrappings clash with each other.
On one side, the lonely heartless villas of the guards.
Dustbins stored like sandbags outside barrackrooms.
The play of searchlights . . . On the other, *Der Neue
Tag* dawns only twice a week nowadays. With its
Nazi-sounding name and millenarian ideals, still
holding the fort for a dwindling readership . . .

Birds of Passage

'The slash of rain. Outside the window, blackbirds
shoot around like dark clouds in the sycamore.
It is meat and drink to them. Between its leaves,
the sky is silver paper, the end of their world . . .

I stare away. I don't want to watch the circus
of my husband's homecoming, a bankrupt show
of defensiveness, guilt and irritability . . .
Two routes in his head, two itineraries, two women.'

Extinction

So now, after twenty-six years, he hangs up
and walks out on you. The line goes dead
as you tell me. Electricity cheeps and thrills—
a malfunction at some international exchange.

There wasn't time to offer sympathy or advice,
not that I knew what to say, in any case . . .
Your life has been one attrition, and when you try
clumsily to defend your interests, he snaps back:

"Forward my mail, I'm not coming home again."
For him, as for the Old Man of the Sea,
there's always someone else, another willing back
to climb. But when you're a woman, past fifty,

with a family and no career, what then . . . ?
Flat earth, the narrative curve of dusk.
A string of lights indicates the road that
brings people to this place. The rip of canvas

as pigeons scatter in terror from their branches.
A faraway siren sounds like faint breathing.
From the middle of a field, the plaintive
squeak of some low and resilient life-form . . .

Pastorale

(for Beat Sterchi)

Where the cars razored past on the blue highway,
I walked, unreasonably, *contre-sens*,

the slewed census-taker on the green verge,
noting a hedgehog's defensive needle-spill,

the bullet-copper and bullet-steel of pheasants,
henna ferns and a six-pack of *Feminax*,

indecipherable cans and the cursive snout and tail
of a flattened rat under the floribund ivy,

the farmer's stockpiled hayrolls and his flocks—
ancillary, bacillary blocks of anthrax.

On Fanø

Acid rain from the Ruhr strips one pine in three . . .
To supplement their living, the neutral Danes
let out their houses during the summer months—
exposure, convexity, clouds and the shadows of clouds.
Wild grass grows on the manure of their thatch.

There are concrete bunkers among the sand dunes—
bomb shelters, or part of Heligoland and the V2s . . . ?
German hippies have taken them over, painted them
with their acid peace dreams; a cave art of
giant people, jungles, a plague of dragonflies.

Summer '87

I was lying out on the caesium lawn,
on the ribs and ligatures of a split deckchair,
under the Roman purple of a copper beech,
a misgrown fasces, all rods and no axe.

It was the double-zero summer, where the birds
stunned themselves on the picture windows
with no red bird cardboard cutout doubles to warn them,
where the puffball dandelion grew twice as high,

where it was better not to eat parsley.
Every Friday, the newspapers gave fresh readings,
and put Turkish hazelnuts on the index.
A becquerel might be a fish or a type of mushroom.

In Munich, cylindrical missile balloons
bounced table-high, head-high, caber-high, house-high.
The crowds on the Leopoldstrasse were thick as pebbles
on the beach. I lay out on the caesium lawn.

Shapes of Things

We are living in the long shadow of the Bomb—
a fat Greenpeace whale, simplified and schematic
like the sign "lavatories for the handicapped",
its whirling genitals a small outboard swastika . . .

I saw the rare Ava Gardner, the last woman alive,
modelling her check workshirts in *On the Beach*.
As the wind drove the heavy clouds of fallout
towards them, there were no ugly scenes of anarchy—

only revivalist preachers and the Salvation Army band . .
She admired the *esprit de corps* of her husband
as he went down in the last living submarine—
an obsolete nuclear cigar, doused in the bay.

On the Beach at Thorpeness

I looked idly right for corpses in the underbrush,
then left, to check that Sizewell was still there.
The wind was from that quarter, northeasterly, a seawind,
B-wind, from that triune reliable fissile block.

—It blackened the drainage ditches
on the low coastal plain, blew up a dry tushing rustle
from the liberal-democratic Aesopian bullrushes,
and an ill-tempered creaking from Christian oaks . . .

A set of three-point lion prints padded up the beach.
The tideline was a ravel of seaweed and detritus,
a red ragged square of John Bull plastic,
a gull's feather lying down by a fishspine.

The North Sea was a yeasty, sudsy brown slop.
My feet jingled on the sloping gravel,
a crisp musical shingle. My tracks were oval holes
like whole notes or snowshoes or Dover soles.

Roaring waves of fighters headed back to Bentwaters.
The tide advanced in blunt codshead curves,
ebbed through the chattering teeth of the pebbles.
Jaw jaw. War war.

Campaign Fever

We woke drugged and naked. Did our flowers
rob us and beat us over the head while we were asleep?
They were competing for the same air as us –
the thick, vegetable breath of under the eaves.

It seems like several days ago that I went
to see you to your train. A cuckoo called
and our vision drizzled, though the air was dry.
In a place I'd never noticed before, a low siren

was sounding alternate notes. I remembered
it had been going all night. Was it in distress?
I slept four times, and ate with the base,
groundless haste of someone eating alone.

Afterwards I smoked a cigarette and lay on my back
panting, as heavy and immobile as my own saliva.
The newspapers preyed on my mind. On the radio,
the National Front had five minutes to put their case.

The fiction of an all-white Albion, deludedness
and control, like my landlady's white-haired old bitch,
who confuses home with the world, pees just inside the door,
and shits trivially in a bend in the corridor.

Mr Thatcher made his pile by clearing railway lines
with sheep-dip (the millionaire's statutory one idea).
When he sold his shares, they grew neglected,
plants break out and reclaim the very pavements . . .

I think of you trundling across Middle England,
Peterborough, Leicester, Birmingham New Street –
the onetime marginals – up to your eyes in a vigorous,
delinquent haze of buttercups, milfoil and maple scrub.

Myopia in Rupert Brooke Country

Birds, feathers, a few leaves, flakes of soot—
things start to fall. The stubble has been burned,
and the fields are striped in black and gold.
Elsewhere, the hay is still drying on long racks:
bulky men prancing about on slender hooves,
unconvincing as pantomime cattle . . . A hedgehog
lies rolled over on its side like a broken castor.
Abandoned in one corner is a caravan that has
not been on holiday all year. Forever England . . .
A hot-air balloon sinks towards the horizon—
the amateur spirit or an advertising gimmick?
Quickly flames light it up, the primitive roar
of a kitchen geyser, and its calcified heart
gives a little skip, then slides down like tears.

In the Realm of the Senses

One perfunctory fuck on our first night,
then nothing for ever . . . only jokes and hard lines,
cold water, mushy soap and sleep that never comes.
We hurt with tiredness, and are abashed by our dirt.

We fall further behind the days, our overnighted systems
struggle with smoke and sights and *consommations*.
The yellow Citroën sits up and fills its lungs,
a black and white green-backed mongrel sees us off.

The road skirts the airport like a stray runway.
Incoming planes make as if to pick us off.
Sometimes it divides: one half runs along the ground,
the other makes a sudden hump – my fear of flyovers.

A little further, I read the simple-minded vertical lettering
on *Ariane*, the unmanned European rocket, the harmless beige
skin-tone of *café au lait*, falling back to earth
in eighty seconds, no use even to the weatherman . . .

We return late at night, my eyes are on stalks,
the breeze whips them into stiff peaks of inflammation
as they stare and stare at the city lights, *Gruppensex*,
Naked Encounter, the breasts a woman bared to cool . . .

Our cat has sprayed the house to greet us.
Lust hurts him into eloquence, almost speech –
like the rabble-rousing live music on the record player,
cynical, manipulative, knowing where it wants to go.

Too tense for sex, too slow to kill, nothing
is as loud as the throbbing duet of the pigeons
in their bay on the roof, as the hours he spent
trapped in a thorn-bush, inhaling a local beauty.

Eclogue

Industry undressing in front of Agriculture –
not a pretty sight. The subject for one
of those allegorical Victorian sculptures.
An energetic mismatch. But Pluto's hell-holes
terminate in or around the flower-meadows
and orchards of Proserpine. Ceres's poor daughter
is whisked away by the top-hatted manufacturer
on his iron horse . . . Brick huts in the fields,
barred mine entrances from the last century,
narrow-gauge railways, powdery cement factories.
A quarry is an inverted cathedral: witchcraft,
a steeple of air sharpened and buried in the ground.
– All around these dangerous sites, sheep graze,
horned and bleating like eminent Victorians.

Nighthawks

(for James Lasdun)

Time isn't money, at our age, it's water.
You couldn't say we cupped our hands very tightly . . .
We missed the second-last train, and find ourselves
at the station with half an hour to kill.

The derelicts queue twice round the tearoom.
Outside, the controlled prostitutes move smoothly
through the shoals of men laughing off their fear.
The street-lamps are a dull coral, snakes' heads.

Earlier, I watched a couple over your shoulder.
She was thin, bone-chested, dressed in black lace,
her best feature vines of hair. Blatant, ravenous,
post-coital, they greased their fingers as they ate.

I met a dim acquaintance, a man with the manner
of a laughing-gas victim, rich, frightened and jovial.
Why doesn't everyone wear pink, he squeaked.
Only a couple of blocks are safe in his world.

Now we've arrived at this hamburger heaven,
a bright hole walled with mirrors where our faces show
pale and evacuated in the neon. We spoon our sundaes
from a metal dish. The chopped nuts are poison.

We've been six straight hours together, my friend,
sitting in a shroud of earnestness and misgiving.
Swarthy, big-lipped, suffering, tubercular,
your hollow darkness survives even in this place . . .

48

The branch-line is under the axe, but it still runs,
rattling and screeching, between the hospital
lit like a toy, and the castellated factory –
a *folie de grandeur* of late capitalism.

Albion Market

Warm air and no sun – the sky was like cardboard,
the same depthless no-colour as the pavements and buildings.
It was May, and pink cherry blossoms lay and shoaled
in the gutter, bleeding as after some wedding . . .

Broken glass, corrugated tin and spraygunned plywood
saying
Arsenal rules the world. Twenty floors up Chantry Point,
the grey diamond panels over two arsoned windows
were scorched like a couple of raised eyebrows.

Tireless and sick, women hunted for bargains.
Gold and silver were half-price. Clothes shops
started up, enjoyed a certain vogue, then
went into a tailspin of permanent sales,

cutting their throats. A window waved *Goodbye, Kilburn*,
and *Everything Must Go*. The *Last Day* was weeks ago –
it didn't. The tailor's became *Rock Bottom*.
On the pavement, men were selling shoelaces.

A few streets away, in the renovated precinct,
girls' names and numbers stood on every lamp-post,
phone-booth, parking meter and tree. Felt tip on sticky
labels,
'rubber', and 'correction' for the incorrigible.

At night, the taxis crawled through Bayswater,
where women dangled their 'most things considered' from
the kerb.
A man came down the street with the meth-pink eyes
of a white rat, his gait a mortal shuffle.

A British bulldog bowler hat clung to his melting skull.
. . . Game spirits, tat and service industries,
an economy stripped to the skin trade. Sex and security,
Arsenal boot boys, white slaves and the SAS.

From Kensal Rise to Heaven

Old Labour slogans, *Venceremos*, dates for demonstrations
like passed deadlines – they must be disappointed
to find they still exist. Halfway down the street,
a sign struggles to its feet and says Brent.

The surfaces are friable, broken and dirty, a skin unsuitable
for chemical treatment. Building, repair and demolition
go on simultaneously, indistinguishably. Change and decay.
– When change is arrested, what do you get?

The Sun, our Chinese takeaway, is being repainted.
I see an orange topcoat calls for a pink undercoat.
A Chinese calendar girl, naked, chaste and varnished,
simpers behind potplants like a jungle dawn.

Joy, local, it says in the phone-booth, with a number
next to it. Or *Petra*. Or *Out of Order*, and an arrow.
This last gives you pause, ten minutes, several weeks . . .
Delay deters the opportunist as much as doubt.

In an elementary deception, the name of the street
is taken from a country town, and when I get up
I find my education is back to haunt me: Dickens House,
Blake Court, Austen House, thirteen-storey giants.

Some Sunday mornings, blood trails down the street
from the night before. Stabbing, punch-up or nosebleed,
it's impossible to guess, but the drops fell thickly and easily
on the paving-stones, too many for the rules of hopscotch.

The roadway itself is reddish, the faded spongy brick
of the terrace is overpowered by the paintwork's
sweet dessert colours. They spoil it, but you understand
they are there as the sugar in tomato soup is there.

Clouds come over from the West, as always in England
the feeling that the sea is just beyond the next horizon:
a thick, Byzantine crucifix on a steep schoolhouse roof,
the slippery, ecclesiastical gleam of wet slate.

Dogs vet the garbage before the refuse collectors.
Brazen starlings and pigeons, 'flying rats', go over
what is left. Rough-necked, microcephalous, they have
too much white on their bodies, like calcium defectives.

The pigeons mate in full view: some preliminary billing,
then the male flutters his wings as though to break a
                                        fall . . .
They inhabit a ruined chiropodist's, coming and going freely
through broken windows into their cosy excremental hollow.

The old man in the vest in the old people's home
would willingly watch us all day. In their windows,
a kind of alcove, they keep wine bottles and candlesticks,
Torvill and Dean, a special occasion on ice.

The motor-mews has flat roofs of sandpaper or tarpaper.
One is terraced, like three descending trays of gravel.
Their skylights are angled towards the red East,
some are truncated pyramids, others whole glazed shacks.

Open House

Rawlplugs and polyfilla . . . the cheerful,
tamping thump of reggae through the floorboards,

the drawling vowel 'r' of Irish or Jamaican English
carrying easily through the heated, excitable air –

as though I lived in a museum without walls.

Dean Point

It was some kind of quarry, a great excavation—
caterpillar treads, surface water, lumps of clay,
the mess of possibilities . . . It bore the forbidden,
almost criminal aspect of industrial premises.

Ramps led down from one level circle to another,
three or four turns of a gigantic blunt screw.
Corrugated iron towers passed among themselves
on conveyor belts whatever was produced there,

and there was a blue-water harbour where it might be
transported along the coast, or to another coast.
We couldn't have told it from by-product or waste.
The soft rock fell to pieces in my hands.

To one side was a beach, with stones and trash.
Spongy sea plants grew on it, and what looked like
bloodied thighbones but were only a different seaweed.
The sea spilt itself a little way onto the grey sand.

Part III

Day of Reckoning

When we drove across America, going West,
I tanned through the sandwich glass windscreen.
Though I was eight, and my legs weren't yet long
in their long pants, I could still sit in front –

your co-driver who couldn't spell you . . .
My jagged elbow stuck out of the right-hand window,
I kept a tough diary, owned a blunt knife,
and my mother sat in the back with the girls.

I can't remember if we talked, or if, even then,
you played the radio, but when I got tired
I huddled in my legroom in the Chevy Belair,
and watched the coloured stars under the dashboard . . .

I learned fractions from you in a single day,
multiplying and dividing. In Kingston, Ontario,
I had a cruel haircut. For you, it was a dry time –
in two years one short play about bankruptcy:

Let Them Down, Gently. There followed the great crash.

The Machine That Cried

'Il n'y a pas de détail'–Paul Valéry

When I learned that my parents were returning
to Germany, and that I was to be jettisoned,
I gave a sudden lurch into infancy and Englishness.
Carpets again loomed large in my world: I sought out
their fabric and warmth, where there was nowhere to fall . . .

I took up jigsaw puzzles, read mystical cricket thrillers
passing all understanding, even collected toy soldiers
and killed them with matchsticks fired from the World War
                                                            One
field-guns I bought from Peter Oborn down the road
– he must have had something German, with that name –

who lived alone with his mother, like a man . . .
My classmates were equipped with sexual insults
for the foaming lace of the English women playing
                                                    Wimbledon,
but I watched them blandly on our rented set
behind drawn curtains, without ever getting the point.

My building-projects were as ambitious as the Tower of
                                                            Babel.
Something automotive of my construction limped across the
                                                            floor
to no purpose, only lugging its heavy battery.
Was there perhaps some future for Christiaan Barnard,
or the electric car, a milk-float groaning like a sacred heart?

I imagined Moog as von Moog, a mad German scientist.
His synthesizer was supposed to be the last word in
                                        versatility,
but when I first heard it on Chicory Tip's
Son of my Father, it was just a unisono metallic drone,
five notes, as inhibited and pleonastic as the title.

My father bought a gramophone, a black box,
and played late Beethoven on it, which my mother was always
to associate with her miscarriage of that year.
I was forever carrying it up to my room,
and quietly playing through my infant collection of singles,

Led Zeppelin, The Tremoloes, *My Sweet Lord* . . .
The drums cut like a scalpel across the other instruments.
Sometimes the turntable rotated slowly, then everything
went flat, and I thought how with a little more care
it could have been all right. There again, so many things

were undependable . . . My first-ever British accent wavered
between Pakistani and Welsh. I called *Bruce's* record shop
just for someone to talk to. He said, 'Certainly, Madam.'
Weeks later, it was 'Yes sir, you can bring your children.'
It seemed I had engineered my own birth in the new country.

Family Holidays

The car got a sun-tan while my father worked
in its compound . . . Mixed with the cicadas,
you could hear the fecundity of his typing
under the green corrugated plastic roof.

My mother staggered about like a nude
in her sun-hat, high heels and bathing-costume.
She was Quartermaster and Communications.

My doughy sisters baked on the stony beach,
swelling out of their bikinis, turning over
every half-hour. Still, they were never done.

The little one fraternized with foreign children.

. . . Every day I swam further out of my depth,
but always, miserably, crawled back to safety.

My Father's House Has Many Mansions

Who could have said we belonged together,
my father and my self, out walking, our hands held
behind our backs in the way Goethe recommended?

Our heavy glances tipped us forward – the future,
a wedge of pavement with our shoes in it . . .
In your case, beige, stacked, echoing clogs;

and mine, the internationally scruffy tennis shoes –
seen but not heard – of the protest movement.
My mother shook her head at us from the window.

I was taller and faster but more considerate:
tense, overgrown, there on sufferance, I slowed down
and stooped for you. I wanted to share your life.

Live with you in your half-house in Ljubljana,
your second address: talk and read books;
meet your girl-friends, short-haired, dark, oral;

go shopping with cheap red money in the supermarket;
share the ants in the kitchen, the unfurnished rooms,
the fallible winter plumbing. Family was abasement

and obligation . . . The three steps to your door
were three steps to heaven. But there were only visits.
At a party for your students – my initiation! –

I ceremoniously downed a leather glass of *slivovica*.
But then nothing. I wanted your mixture of resentment
and pride in me expanded to the offer of equality.

Is the destination of paternity only advice . . . ?
In their ecstasy of growth, the bushes along the drive
scratch your bodywork, dislocate your wing-mirror.

Every year, the heraldic plum-tree in your garden
surprises you with its small, rotten fruit.

Bärli

Your salami breath tyrannized the bedroom
where you slept on the left, my mother, tidily,
on the right. I could cut the atmosphere with a knife:

the enthusiasm for spice, rawness, vigour,
in the choppy air. It was like your signature,
a rapid scrawl from the side of your pen –

individual, overwhelming, impossible –
a black Greek energy that cramped itself into
affectionate diminutives, *Dein Vati*, or *Papi*.

At forty, you had your tonsils out, child's play
with Little Bear nuns, Ursulines for nurses.
Hours after the operation, you called home . . .

humbled and impatient, you could only croak.
I shivered at your weakness – the faint breeze
that blew through you and formed words.

Lighting Out

Business, independence, a man alone, travelling –
I was on your territory. Though what I represented
was not myself, but a lawnmower manufacturer,
whipping round the green belts in Northern Germany.

Hardly your line, then – that would have been
a tour of radio stations, or public readings –
but once I swanned off to mercantile Lübeck, and saw
Thomas Mann's ugly Nobel plaque, and the twin towers

on fifty-mark banknotes. And I coincided
with the publication of your firstborn, *The Denunciation*.
I proudly bought a copy on my expenses, giving you
your first royalties on twenty-odd years of my life . . .

But being a salesman was dispiriting work. I ran myself
like an organization, held out the prospect of bonuses,
wondered which of the tiny, sad, colourful bottles
in my freezing minibar I would crack next.

Gruppenbild ohne Dame

1923, gathering Depression. In this interior
in Cologne, it's Laocöon all over again.
This time, Fate has left him his two boys
and taken his wife.—Though it is difficult
to see how a woman could have fitted in, here:
a road winding in an empty landscape on the wall,
the threadbare carpet, and one hard Sunday chair.
. . . A male Trinity, the Father and his two Sons.
The maculate conceptions of his bald head.
Baby watchchains like Papa's, and knickerbockers
aspiring to the condition of his three-piece suit.
Their knotty skulls show a family likeness,
heads shaved for lice and summer—skinny boys
with their mother's big eyes and hurt mouth.

The Means of Production

Like a man pleading for his life,
you put novels between yourself
and your pursuers – Atalanta,
always one step ahead of the game.

You gave me a copy of your second
with the dedication: *Michael,*
something else for you to read.
Your disparaging imperative

was too much resented for obedience . . .
You were a late starter at fiction,
but for ten years now, your family
has been kept at arm's length.

– We are as the warts on your elbows,
scratched into submission, but always
recrudescent. You call each of us
child, your wife and four children,

three of them grown-up. You have
the biblical manner: the indulgent patriarch,
his abused, endless patience; smiling
the absent smile of inattention . . .

Everything you need is at your desk:
glue-stained typewriter, match-sticks,
unravelled paper-clips – *Struwwelpeter* props!
With your big work-scissors, you snipe

at your nails, making the sparks fly.
The radio updates its bulletins
every hour, guarding you against surprises.
The living breath of the contemporary . . .

Once, you acceded to conversation,
got up to put on your black armband
and took your blood-pressure, as though
in the presence of an unacceptable risk.

The Magic of Mantovani

(for Simon Korner)

The invited audience applauds on cue—
steady couples in their late twenties,
well-dressed and supplied with contraceptives.

A giant in the world of light music, they say;
so much happiness in those globe-trotting tunes . . .
The surf of percussion. Swaying in treetops,

violins hold the high notes. Careful brass
for the darker moments—the blood of Spain.
The accordion is a European capital . . .

A sentimental music, porous with associations,
it played in the dimness before the ads,
when I went to the cinema with my father.

He disappeared into his own thoughts, abstracted,
rubbing his fingers together under his nose . . .
Scattered in the red plush of the cinema,

a handful of people were waiting for the feature.
Regular constellations of stars twinkled
on the ceiling while daylight wasted outside.

Ice-cream was no longer on sale in the foyer—
the end of kindness . . . I thought about mortality,
and cried for my father's inevitable death.

Vortex

Where was our high-water mark? Was it the glorious
oriental scimitar in the Metropolitan Museum
in New York? Nothing for a pussyfooting shake-hands grip:
your hand had to be a fist already to hold it . . .
I wondered why the jewels were all clustered
on scabbard and hilt and basketed hand-guard,
why there were none on the sword itself.
I could only guess that the blade leapt out
to protect them, like a strong father his family.

– Or next door, where, as the guide explained,
there was a deity in the ceiling, who would shower
genius or intellect or eyewash on those beneath?
And straightaway, to my fierce embarrassment,
you pushed me under it, an un-European moment –
though I tried also to relish the shiver of limelight.

– Or was it more even, less clinching, the many years
I used the basin after you had shaved in it?
It was my duty to shave the basin, rinsing
the circle of hairs from its concave enamel face
till it was as smooth as yours . . . I was almost there,
on the periphery of manhood, but I didn't have your gear:
the stiff brush of real badger (or was it beaver?);
the reserved cake of shaving soap; the safety razor
that opened like Aladdin's cave when I twirled the handle.
. . . That movement became an escape mechanism:
I was an orphan, a street Arab, waiting for you
in international lounges, at the foot of skyscrapers;
entertaining myself with the sprinkler nozzles
secreted in the ceiling, whirling dervishes
sniffing out smoke, in a state of permanent readiness;
or with the sprung, centrifugal, stainless ashtrays
that have since emancipated me, like the razors
– cheapskate, disposable, no moving parts –
I now use myself . . . The water drains away, laughing.
I light up, a new man.

Withdrawn from Circulation

My window gave on to a street-corner where the air currents
(*Berliner Luft!*) were of such bewildering complexity
that the snow, discouraged, fell back up the sky . . .

It stayed shut, and I sweated in the central heat
as I sweated in my pyjamas at night, snug as a worm
in my slithery tapering orange-and-green sleeping bag.

For a whole month, the one soiled bedsheet
was supposed to knit together, to join in matrimony
the shiny blue tripartite mattress, borrowed or looted

from a ruined office, but good as new.
Small wonder I hugged it in sleep! On the floor
lay the door that was to have made me a table.

It was said there was nothing between here and Siberia –
except Poland – but indoors was the tropics.
I was eighteen, and frittering away.

I picked up just enough politics to frighten my mother,
and the slick, witless phrases I used about girls
were a mixture of my father's and those I remembered

from *Mädchen* or *Bravo* . . . Nothing quite touched me.
I put on weight, smoked Players and read Dickens
for anchorage and solidity. Come the autumn,

I was going to Cambridge. A few doors down
was the cellar where the RAF kept the Berlin Senator
they had kidnapped and were holding to ransom.

From time to time, his picture appeared
in the newspapers, authenticated by other newspapers
in the picture with him. He was news that stayed news.

Giro Account

Out of the pornographic cinema at the station,
with the fast clock and the continuous programme,
then past the French sweet-stall, the naturist magazines

and the cretin at the lottery ticket-office
– *das schnelle Glück*: a quick buck or fuck –
and into the night train to Berlin . . .

It was sealed and non-stop, but East German border guards
woke us up so they could give us our transit visas,
and then it was early on Sunday, and I walked

out of *Berlin-Zoo* in my father's lion coat,
his suitcase in one hand and his bag in the other.
I was nineteen and a remittance man,

embarked on a delirium of self-sufficiency,
surprised that it was possible to live like a bird:
to stay in a hotel, to eat in restaurants,

and draw my father's money from a giro account.
At the end of my feeding-tube, I didn't realize
that to stay anywhere on the earth's surface is to bleed:

money, attention, effort . . . It was no problem.
I avoided my companions – the cold young man
with the Inca cap, the weak heart and the blue face,

his obese, scatologically-brained sister – and stared
incessantly at a Peruvian woman in a night-club.
There was a girl who one day told me she'd become engaged.

The motherly hotel manageress gave me the rolls
left over from my breakfast for the rest of the day.
Once, she gave me my father on the telephone.

I asked him about his conference, but he wanted
something else: to have me at the end of a telephone
line, an alibi, proof of my harmlessness –

he had become jealous of a spivvy young Englishman . . .
There was no crime, no conference, maybe no Englishman:
only my father, his son and his new novel plot.

Catechism

My father peers into the lit sitting-room
and says, 'Are you here?' . . . Yes, I am,
in one of his cloudy white leather armchairs,
with one foot not too disrespectfully on the table,
reading Horváth's *Godless Youth*. Without another word,
he goes out again, baffling and incommunicable,
the invisible man, dampening any speculation.

My Father at Fifty

Your mysterious economy blows the buttons
off your shirts, and permits overdrafts
at several foreign banks. – It must cost the earth.

Once I thought of you virtually as a savage,
atavistic, well-aligned, without frailties.
A man of strong appetites, governed by instinct.

You never cleaned your teeth, but they were perfect anyway
from a diet of undercooked meat; you gnawed the bones;
anything sweet you considered frivolous.

Your marvellous, single-minded régime, kept up
for years, of getting up at four or five,
and writing a few pages 'on an empty stomach',

before exposing yourself to words – whether
on the radio, in books or newspapers,
or just your own from the day before . . .

Things are different now. Your male discriminations
– meat and work – have lost their edge.
Your teeth are filled, an omnivorous sign.

Wherever you are, there is a barrage of noise:
your difficult breathing, or the blaring radio –
as thoughtless and necessary as breathing.

You have gone to seed like Third World dictators,
fat heads of state suffering horribly
from Western diseases whose name is Legion . . .

Your concentration is gone: every twenty minutes,
you go to the kitchen, or you call your wife
over some trifle. Bad-tempered and irritable,

you sedate yourself to save the energy
of an outburst. Your kidneys hurt, there is even
a red band of eczema starring your chest.

Your beard – the friend of the writer who doesn't smoke –
is shot with white . . . A Christmas card arrives
to ask why you don't have any grandchildren.

Author, Author

'verba volant, scripta manent'

Can this be all that remains – two or three weeks a year,
sitting at the opposite end of the dinner table from my
father?

To listen to his breathing, more snorting than breathing,
puffing out air through his nose during mouthfuls,

chewing loudly with open mouth, without enjoyment,
uninhibited, inhibiting, his only talk, talk of food?

And to watch myself watching him, fastidious and disloyal,
feeling my muscles through my shirt – an open knife!

(My own part of the conversation, thin, witty, inaudible,
as though I'd spoken in asides for twenty-five years.)

To come back to him unannounced, at regular intervals,
one of two or three unselfsufficient, cryptic,

grown-up strangers he has fathered, and see again
his small silver mouth in his great grizzled face,

head and stomach grown to childlike proportions,
supported on his unchanging, teenager's legs . . .

To come upon by chance, while emptying the dustbin,
the ripped, glittery foil-wrapping of his heart-medicines,

multiplication times-tables of empty capsules,
dosages like police ammunition in a civil disturbance,

bought for cash over the counter and taken according to
need –
like his sudden peremptory thirst for a quart of milk.

If sex is nostalgia for sex, and food nostalgia for food,
his can't be – what did a child of the War get to eat

that he would want to go on eating, and to share?
Standing in the road as the American trucks rolled by:

chewing-gum, cigarettes, canned herrings, a kick in the
teeth.
(The way it is with dogs, and their first puppy nourishment:

potato-peelings, or my maternal grandmother in East
Germany,
and Chéri, her gay dog – pampered, shy, neurotic Chéri,

corrupted by affection, his anal glands spoiling with
virginity –
she feeds him heart and rice, the only cooking she ever
does.) . . .

After the age of fifty, a sudden flowering, half a dozen
novels
in as many years – dialogue by other means: his main
characters

maniacs, compulsive, virtuoso talkers, talkers for dear life,
talkers in soliloquies, notebooks, tape-recordings, last
wills . . .

Hear him on the telephone, an overloud, forced bonhomie,
standing feet crossed, and one punishing the other for
lying,

woken up once at midnight by a drunken critic
with his girl-friend hanging on the extension –

her sweet name not a name at all, but a blandishment –
finishing with promises, and his vestigial phrase of English

after ten years in England, *'Bye, bye.'* Then going off to pee,
like the boys at my boarding-school after fire-practice . . .

Till that time, I had a worshipful proximity with him,
companionable and idolatrous. If my nose wasn't hooked,

my hair not black and straight, my frame too long,
my fingers not squat and powerful, fitting the typewriter keys,

then it was my mother's fault, her dilution, her adulteration.
Home from England, I landed on a checkered pattern

of unwillingness and miserable advice. Not to take drugs,
not to treat my face with vinegar or lemon-juice,

to make influential friends, and not to consort with others.
And, on interesting subjects, either a silence

or the interviewee's too-rapid turning to his own
                                    experience . . .
Perplexed, wounded, without confidence, I left him to
                                    himself,

first going round the block on a small-wheeled bicycle
in one of his leather jackets, like an elderly terror;

or, now, on walks with my mother in the shitty park
among the burghers: his duffle-coat in the zoo of democracy.

A performance, like everything else . . . What's the point?
He wants only his car and his typewriter and his Magic
                                                      Marker.

Every action he divides into small stages, every traffic light
on the way home, and each one he punctuates with a
                                          crucified 'So.'

I ask myself what sort of consummation is available?
Fight; talk literature and politics; get drunk together?

Kiss him goodnight, as though half my life had never
                                          happened?

The Late Richard Dadd, 1817–1886

The *Kentish Independent* of 1843
carried his pictures of his father, himself
and the scene of his crime. The first photojournalist:
fairy-painter, father-slayer, poor, bad, mad Richard Dadd.

His extended Grand Tour took in the Holy Land
and ended in Bethlem Hospital, with its long panoptical
galleries, spider plants, whippets and double gaslights.
He had outlived himself at twenty-six . . .

There was one day he seemed to catch sunstroke.
He fancied the black, scorched beard of a sheik
would furnish him with some 'capital paintbrushes.'
Sailing up the Nile, on the *Hecate,*

they spent Christmas Day eating boiled eggs
and plum pudding, and playing cards for the captain's soul.
The temples at Luxor stood under a full moon, lightly
                                            boiled.
Sir Thomas got off to try and bag a crocodile.

The route up from Marseille went as the crow flies—
precipitately, a dash from ear to ear.
A fellow traveler let him play with his collar and tie,
until he pulled out 'an excellent English razor.'

There was his watercolour, *Dead Camel,*
and a series of drawings of his friends,
all with their throats cut,
Frith, Egg, Dadd, Phillip and O'Neill.

He saw himself as a catspaw, Osiris's right-hand man
on earth. His digs in Newman Street
contained three hundred eggs, and the earth
cracked when he walked on it.

Fine Adjustments

By now, it is almost my father's arm,
a man's arm, that lifts the cigarettes to my mouth
numbed by smoke and raw onions and chocolate milk.

I need calm, something to tranquillize me
after the sudden storm between us that left me shaking,
and with sticky palms . . . It only happens here,

where I blurt in German, dissatisfied and unproficient
amid the material exhilaration of abstract furniture,
a new car on the Autobahn, electric pylons walking

through the erasures in the Bayrischer Wald . . .
Once before, I left some lines of Joseph Roth
bleeding on your desk: *'I had no father – that is,*

I never knew my father – but Zipper had one.
That made my friend seem quite privileged,
as though he had a parrot or a St Bernard.'

All at once, my nature as a child hits me.
I was a moving particle, like the skidding lights
in a film-still. Provoking and of no account,

I kept up a constant rearguard action, jibing,
commenting, sermonizing. 'Why did God give me a voice,'
I asked, 'if you always keep the radio on?'

It was a fugitive childhood. Aged four, I was chased
round and round the table by my father, who fell
and broke his arm he was going to raise against me.

Old Firm

Father, the writer bird writes bird's-nest soup—
a frail, disciplined structure, spun from its spittle
with bits of straw and dirt, then boiled with beaten eggs . . .
It kept us fed till we were big enough to leave the nest.

We walked, *à trois*, to the end of the road, for my bus
to Riem, and the plane to Gatwick, seemingly
chartered by the *Bierfest* . . . A sudden thunderstorm
turned us into a family group: mother under her umbrella,

you hiding in a phone-box, kindly holding the door open,
and me, giving no protection, and pretending
not to seek any either, wet and deserting and plastered,
like the hair making itself scarce on your bad head . . .

That morning you played me an interview you gave in French,
a language you hadn't spoken in my lifetime,
literally not since my birth, when you'd been in Toulouse,
on French leave . . . Now, we joked about it –

you were easier to understand than the interviewer!
Who else understood? Your edgy, defeated laugh?
The modest, unhopeful evangelism of your final appeal
to the people of Montreal not to stop reading?

Lament for Crassus

Who grows old in fifty pages of Plutarch:
mores, omens, campaigns, Marius at sixty,
fighting fit, working out on the Campus Martius?

It surely isn't me, pushing thirty, taking a life a night,
my head on a bookshelf, five shelves of books overhead,
the bed either a classic or remaindered?

—I read about Crassus, who owned most of Rome.
Crassus, the third man, the third triumvir,
the second term in any calculation.

Crassus, the pioneer of insuranburn,
with his architect slaves and firefighter slaves,
big in silver, big in real estate, big in personnel.

Crassus, who had his name linked with a Vestal Virgin,
but was only after her house in the suburbs.
Crassus of bread and suburbs and circuses,

made Consul for his circuses, Crassus
impresario, not Crassus *imperator*, Crassus
who tried to break the military-political nexus.

Crassus, the inventor of the demi-pension holiday,
holed up in a cave on the coast of Spain for a month,
getting his dinner put out for him, and a couple of slave-
                                                        girls.

Crassus, whose standards wouldn't rise on the final day,
who came out of his corner in careless black,
whose head, when severed, was a day younger than his
                                                        son's.

Part IV   (ENDZEIT)

White Noise

It blows your mind,

the radio, or whatever piece of sonic equipment
you keep along with the single white rose
and the spiked mirror in your monochrome room . . .
I've seen it through the open door sometimes.

You hoover twice a week, and in my eyes
that amounts to a passion for cleanliness.
The vacuum, its pre-war drone in the corridor.
Thin and snub-nosed, a gas-mask on a stick.

Your reveille is at six: you go downstairs
for a glass of water with your vitamin pills.
Then back to your room, and your light stays on
till late.—What do you do to kill the time?

. . . Trailing cigarette smoke and suspicion,
you prowl through the house, accident-prone
and painfully thin in your sepulchral clothes.
Reality filters through your tinted spectacles.

And in the afternoon, your looped-tape excesses:
a couple of pop standards in your repertoire,
the demonstration piece for synthesizer,
and that thrilling concerto for nose-flute . . .

Two floors away, I can still hear the storm.
The jungle and the platitudes of sentiment
battle it out with technology, sweep you
into a corner of your room, delirious, trembling,

a pile of leaves.

Against Nature

Des Esseintes himself would have admired
her fastidiousness – anorexia, years in hospital –
as he gloated over his own peptone enemas . . .
Her horror is a purely physical matter.
If she had her way, it would all cease.

Like sticks of furniture swathed in sheets,
her limbs ghost about the place, longing for peace,
disuse. She walks fast to lose weight –
a blue streak, hoping for invisibility
behind '60s dyed hair and false eyelashes.

In a gesture of self-betrayal, she goes shopping:
powdered milk, Gitanes, cans of cat food
to placate Sappho, her black panther of a cat . . .
A Japanese lodger lived there for a while.
In his country, there are many centenarians –

rice, raw fish, and the subjugation of women
combine to promote longevity in the male.
A dietary expert, he drank as much beer
in an evening as a special *kobe* beef cow.
He never cleaned the bath, and left rich stains

in the lavatory bowl, like a dirty protest . . .
She has a boyfriend of sorts, weird, well-spoken,
Jesus-bearded. His childhood squints from one eye.
Something out of Dostoevsky, he wears only
navy blue – the colour of religious aspirants.

An anonymous depressive, he talks her into knots.
. . . Often, he isn't allowed in to see her.
Then his notes bristle on the doormat like fakirs,
her name on them in big block capitals,
widely spaced on the paranoid envelope . . .

Boys' Own

(i.m. T. J. Park)

A parting slightly off-centre, like Oscar Wilde's,
his fat mouth, and the same bulky appearance.
Your hair was pomaded, an immaculate wet-look,
sculpted and old-fashioned in these blow-dry times.
The dull grain of wood on polished furniture.
—Everyone has an inspiring English teacher
somewhere behind them, and you were ours. We argued
about you: that your smell was not sweet after-shave,
but the presbyterian rigours of cold water—

on your porous face and soft, womanish hands . . . ?
The public-school teacher has to be versatile—
if not the genuine Renaissance article, then at least
a modern pentathlete—and so you appeared to us
in as many guises as an Action Man: for lessons,
with a gown over one of your heavy three-piece suits;
wearing khaki for Corps on Wednesday afternoons;
as a soccer referee in a diabolical black tracksuit;
in baggy but respectable corduroys on holidays . . .

Morning coffee was followed by pre-prandial sherry
after only the shortest of intervals. The empties,
screw-tops, stood in boxes outside your door.
You drank early, copiously, and every day—
though it hardly crossed our minds. Given the chance,
we would have done too . . . It was "civilized",
and that was what you were about. Sweet and sour sherry,
lager on warm afternoons, the pathos of sparkling wine
for occasions. "It's actually quite like champagne . . ."

Just as an extension-lead went from your gramophone
to its little brother, a "stereophonic" loudspeaker—
Ferguson Major and Minor . . . With one hand in your
                                                            pocket,
leaning back in your swivelling chair, you conducted
your own records, legs double-crossed like Joyce's.
—Among all those other self-perpetuating oddball
bachelors, how could we fail to understand you?
Your military discipline and vintage appearance,
the sublimation of your Anglicanism, your drinking . . .

We only waited for that moment at the end of a class,
when, exhausted by intellectual inquiry, you took off
your glasses and rubbed away your tiny blue eyes . . .
All of love and death can be found in books;
you would have agreed. At one of your gatherings,
someone found a pubic hair in your sheepskin rug . . .
Years later, there was a scandal, an ultimatum,
and you threw yourself under the wheels of a train—
the severe way Tolstoy chose for Anna Karenina.

Fates of the Expressionists

The Kaiser was the first cousin of George V,
descended, as he was, from *German* George,
and unhappy Albert, the hard-working Saxon Elector.
—The relaxed, navy-cut beard of the one,
hysterical, bristling moustaches of the other . . .
The Expressionists were Rupert Brooke's generation.
Their hold on life was weaker than a baby's.
Their deaths, at whatever age, were infant mortality—
a bad joke in this century. Suddenly become sleepy,
they dropped like flies, whimsical, sizzling,
ecstatic, from a hot light-bulb. Even before the War,
Georg Heym and a friend died in a skating accident.
From 1914, they died in battle and of disease—
or suicide like Trakl. *Drugs Alcohol Little Sister*.
One was a student at Oxford and died, weeks later,
on the other side . . . Later, they ran from the Nazis.
Benjamin was turned back at the Spanish border—
his history of the streets of Paris unfinished—
deflected into an autistic suicide. In 1938,
Ödön von Horváth, author of naturalistic comedies,
was struck by a falling tree. In Paris.
                                    At the time
my anthology was compiled, there were still a few left:
unexplained survivors,
                        psychoanalysts in the New World.

Max Beckmann: 1915

Nurse, aesthetician and war-artist:
not unpatriotic, not unfeeling.
Calm—excitable. Noted yellow shellholes,
the pink bones of a village steeple, a heated purple sky.
Bombardments. Tricks of the light. Graphic wounds.

An aviator overflew him in the rose night,
buzzed him, performed for him. Friend or foe? *Libellule!*
A room of his own in a villa. *Kriegsblick.*
Medics intellectually stimulating,
one, from Hamburg, familiar with his work.

A commission to decorate the baths
—an Oriental scene, how asinine!—
deserts, palmettoes, oases, dead Anzacs, Dardanelles.
A second fresco, of the bathhouse personnel.
One thousand male nudes per diem.

A prey to faces. Went for a squinting Cranach.
A man with half a head laughed at his sketches,
recognising his companions. (He died today.)
'Several hours' tigerish combat, then gave up
the assault': his description of a sitting.

Some *esprit de corps.* Marching songs
weirdly soothing, took him out of himself.
Ha, the amusing pretensions of a civilian
trying to commandeer a hotel room.
English prisoners, thirsty mudlarks, plucky, droll.

In the trenches the men had kissed their lives goodbye.
A ricochet, a sniper. In the midst of life.
Crosses plugging foxholes, stabbed into sandbags.
A man with a pistol, head down, intent, hunting rats.
Another, frying spuds on a buddy's grave.

The Flemish clocks told German time.
Sekt and Mosel to wash down the yellow *vin de pays*.
Dr. Bonenfant, with his boozy babyface.
'We poor children.' A commission
to illustrate the army songbook. Invalided out.

Wheels

Even the piss-artist, rocking back and forth
on the balls of his feet like a musical policeman,
is making an irreversible commitment . . . He shivers.

(The faith, application and know-how it takes
to do anything, even under controlled circumstances!)
I find in myself this absurd purposefulness;

walking through my house, I lean forward,
I lick my finger to open a door, to turn over a page,
or the page of a calendar, or an advent calendar.

It takes all day to read twenty pages,
and the day goes down in a blaze of television.
One blue day is much like another . . . The plane lands

with a mew of rubber and a few 'less than' signs.
The ball, remembering who hit it, keeps going.
The choreographed car chase is ruinously exciting,

but the wheels turn very slowly backwards,
to convince the viewer that, far from wasting time,
he's recreating himself. A Christmas Special!

From the great outdoors, there's the derision
of real cars, the honeyed drone of approachable taxis,
some man's immortal Jag, numbered RAMISH . . .

How it must cut past the huddle of water-blue Inyacars
lining the elbow of the road: smashed imperatives,
wheelchair hulls, rhombuses, stalled quartz.

This Sporting Death

The days are so dark they hardly count –
but they must have some marginal warmth after all,
for the drizzle of my night-breath turns to fog.

The window is opaque, a white mirror affirming
life goes on inside this damp lung of a room . . .
I have no perspective on the dotty winter clouds,

the pubic scrub of this street I am growing to hate,
with its false burglar alarms and sleeping policemen.
My exhalations blot out the familiar view.

I can tell without looking when your car draws up,
I know its tune as it reaches the end of its tether
and stops under the lamp-post, melodramatic and old-red,

the unwilling gift of your sainted grandmother
who disliked you and died suddenly on Friday.
'Grand-merde' you called her when you left sometimes

to go with her to visit your uncle in hospital,
lying there with irreversible brain damage
almost as long as I've lived here, after

falling downstairs drunk. You chat to him,
and imagine or fail to imagine that he responds
when you play him the recording of his greatest moment

when the horse he trained won the Derby.
I stay here and listen to sport on the radio,
a way of processing time to trial and outcome.

Someone brought me some cigarettes from America
called *Home Run*, and they frighten me half to death
in their innocuous vernal packaging, green and yellow.

Kif

The filter crumples – a cruel exhilaration
as the day's first cigarette draws to a close.
The optician's colours turn to a dizzy whiteness
in my solar plexus . . . With longing I speculate
on Heimito von Doderer's excursus on tobacco –
the pharmaceutical precision of the true scholar.

Disturbances

I go over to my window in South Cambridge,
where the Official Raving Loony Monster candidate
stands to poll half a per cent – the moral majority . . .

Below me, the idyllic lilac tree has scorched
to beehive, to beeswax, to *Bienenstich*, a spongy cack.
Voorman parks his purple car in its shade.

I picture him underneath it, his helter-skelter
fat man jeans halfway down, showing his anal cleft.
Though what would he be doing, face down like that?!

He's even more remote than I am, curtains drawn,
stopping the plug-hole with his hair-loss,
never a letter for him, a visit or a phone-call.

How is it, then, that in the featurelessness
of his Sundays he throws fits, shouting and swearing,
punching the walls, putting us in fear of our lives?

I'm so fearful and indecisive, all my life
has been in education, higher and higher education . . .
What future for the fly with his eye on the flypaper?

The house is breaking up, and still I'm hanging on here:
scaffolding and a skip at the door, smells of dust
and sawdust, the trepanation of the floorboards.

Entropy   (The Late Show)

A split screen, the dream of the early cineastes,
who rounded on their audiences and assaulted them
with pandemonium in a dip- or triptych, shooting
that all-time favourite, the end of the world.
Screaming crowds ensured a box-office success.
People paid to watch themselves and their own
futuristic hysteria in the huge convex mirrors
held up to them in the cinemas of the avant-garde.
They are the antecedents of today's disaster movie
(especially blooming in Japan), and also of this:

game of darts. On the right half of the screen,
completely expressionless, the pot-bellied players.
Standing like storks on one leg, they lean forward
behind their heavy throwing-arm. Some of them use
a little finger as a telescopic sight. They practise
six or seven hours a day . . . On the left, in close-up,
their target, treble twenty. With the best of them,
the margin of error is an eighth of an inch, a letter
in type.
Hating numbers, they rattle down to zero.

Ploughshares

My sheets rode from left to right. Soon I was lying
on the bare security mattress, my arm round a white wraith.
. . . I remembered the film I saw. Wizened and high-cheeked,
the tartar face of Adenauer, first post-war Chancellor,
elected with the margin of one vote, his own. That
was the 'Adenauer era' . . . He warned against Communism
'of the Asiatic type', and said that a free Europe
should extend to the Urals. Improbably, and by subterfuge,
he re-armed Germany (even Strauss, the young outside-right,
wanted 'the arm that held a weapon' to 'drop off'),
and, but for the opposition of the Göttingen professors
and great popular demonstrations, it would have gone nuclear
as well . . . In my dream, the peaceable objects in the larder
flew off, changed their function, their identity,
even, when it was safe to do so, their labels.

Entr'acte

The enemies of democracy were back supporting it.
Soldiers went in fear of their MPs, looked slippy
on the parade ground, tumbling from their personnel carriers,
parleyed in groups of two and three with girls at the gate.

I sat and picnicked on my balcony, no picnic,
eyeing the tarmac through the rusty gridiron underfoot,
flicking ash and wincing at my pips going lickety-split,
hitting the deck fifty feet down, among the sentries . . .

Inside, the wall met neither floor nor ceiling.
Two stripes of light reached into my room from next door,
where I heard an American girl – mezzo, ardent –
crying, 'Don't come, sweet Jesus, not yet.'

A Brief Occupation

(for Gilles)

Six floors up, I found myself like a suicide –
one night, the last thing in a bare room . . .
I was afraid I might frighten my neighbours,
two old ladies dying of terror, thinking
every man was the gasman, every gasman a killer . . .

I was not myself. I was just anyone. The next day,
the place was going to be sold. Every so often,
high-spirited car horns bypassed the dead-end street.
The outside wall was a slowly declining roof,
an electricity meter clung to life by a few threads . . .

There was an inhuman shortage of cloth in that room:
a crocheted rug with a few eloquent hairs on it,
a stone for a pillow, my coat hanging demurely in the
                                                    window.
The hairs belonged to a girl, now back in Greece,
an island, a museum of mankind.

By Forced Marches

Who knows what would happen if you stopped?
The autobiography draws out, lengthens
towards the end. Life stays in one place,
often Rome; and to compensate, you cut up
your time in many pieces. Rations are halved,
then quartered. The emergency is acute.
Now it is one lump of sugar per day.

A Minute's Silence

(i.m. Michael Heffernan)

A seagull murmur or worse—he kept it quiet,
went at his work, made plans. One of his last,
he produced Hugo von Hofmannsthal's fictional
abdication, the Lord Chandos Letter, for radio:
a droll package of Ms and Hs and Fs and Ns—

his, and Hofmannsthal's, and mine, the translator's . . .
The studio was round the corner from Broadcasting House,
in a shakier, worse-favoured building,
hollowed under by the Piccadilly and Victoria Lines
drumming through Regent Street. One minute in three

was useless, a minute's silence, to avoid picking up
the awful judder at the heart of the city . . .
A year on, I'm in a new house and he's dead.
Traffic noises, clean slates hammered down—
to hear the banging, you wouldn't give them a price.

I'm sitting coiled over my letter of condolence,
head down, left elbow out, the verbs tramping stiffly
into the furthest corners of mood and tense, closed
conditionals, Latin and peculiar pluperfects,
like Hofmannsthal's . . . 'I had had no idea . . .'

The Day After

I arrived on a warm day, early, a Sunday.
They were sweeping the gravel dunts of boules,
clearing away the wire rig and char of fireworks.
The red metal ornamental maples, planed and spinning
like globes on stalks, had caught the sun.

The cups of the fountains were running over.
A few drops rolled back on the underside, trailed along,
tense and brimming, and fell into the common pool
like ships going over the edge of the world:
the roaring waters, the stolid, daylong rainbow . . .

It struck eight, nine. There was no wind
to blow the glassy fountains off course. My eyes hurt
from the silver bedding plants and vermillion flowers.
I could almost believe the smooth, slabbed plinth
that said: They will rise again.

Kurt Schwitters in Lakeland

'Like nothing else in Tennessee'
—Wallace Stevens

It was between greens (bowling, cricket),
but the graveyard had stayed immune, half-cut and
                                                  smelling
the yellow, abandoned smell of hay. A couple were casting
dead flowers into a wire trash-coop.

Kurt Schwitters's tombstone was hewn in straight lines,
klipp und klar, in the shape of a hat, brim–crown.
Unseasonable, but undeniably local,
someone had left a dozen daffodils.

The man had flown: a refugee,
then interned on the Isle of Man;
released, dead, exhumed, and returned to Germany,
to vote with his feet for the 1950s.
     •   •   •   •
His *Merz* was nothing to do with pain or March:
it had been withdrawn from the *Kommerz- und Privatbank*.
Each day he caught the early bus to work,
climbed up to his barn through a jungle of rhododendrons,

and built on to his *Merzwall.*—It too was moved,
cased in a steel frame, and keelhauled down the hill.
The one thing still there that his hands had touched
was a stone on the sill

of the picture window that had been put in
in place of the wall. It had an air
of having been given a spin,
a duck, a drakkar, a curling-stone.

About the Author

Michael Hofmann was born in 1957 in Freiburg, West Germany. He moved to England at the age of four and went to schools in Bristol, Edinburgh, and Winchester, with two years in the United States. He studied English at Cambridge and returned to do postgraduate research there, first on Rilke, then on Robert Lowell. Since 1983, he has lived in London as a freelance writer, reviewer, and translator.

Poems by Michael Hofmann first appeared in Volume 5 of Faber's Poetry Introduction series in 1982. His first book, *Nights in the Iron Hotel*, was published by Faber the following year, and his second, *Acrimony* (a Poetry Book Society Choice), in 1986. 'A Minute's Silence' received the Prudence Farmer Prize for best poem in *New Statesman* in 1986; 'On the Beach at Thorpeness' was awarded the same prize in 1988. Hofmann won a Cholmondeley Award in 1984 and the Geoffrey Faber Memorial Prize in 1988.

Hofmann has translated *Castle Gripsholm* by Kurt Tucholsky (1985) and *The Legend of the Holy Drinker* by Joseph Roth (1989, both published by Overlook Press). His translation of a new novel, *Blösch*, by Beat Sterchi, was published by Faber in 1988 and Pantheon in 1990. His version of Brecht's play *The Good Person of Sichuan* was produced at the National Theatre in London in 1989. He is a regular contributor to *London Review of Books* and *Times Literary Supplement*.